MALDON & HEYBRIDGE

THROUGH TIME

Stephen P. Nunn

AMBERLEY PUBLISHING

Maldon Through Time
The dial of a mid-eighteenth-century longcase clock by Maldon horologist John Draper.

First published 2012

Amberley Publishing
The Hill, Stroud
Gloucestershire, GL5 4EP

www.amberley-books.com

Copyright © Stephen P. Nunn, 2012

The right of Stephen P. Nunn to be identified as the Author of this work has been asserted in accordance with the Copyrights, Designs and Patents Act 1988.

ISBN 978 1 84868 074 6

British Library Cataloguing in Publication Data. A catalogue record for this book is available from the British Library.

Typeset in 9.5pt on 12pt Celeste.
Typesetting by Amberley Publishing.
Printed in the UK.

Contents

Acknowledgements

The majority of the old pictures in this book are a product of forty or more years personal collecting. I have happy memories of trips to postcard fairs in my teenage years, accompanied by the late history teacher, Peter Came, and art teacher, Charlie Tait. We always tried to beat each other to 'the best cards' and I hope that my much lamented friends would be proud of this small selection. Many of the modern photographs are my own effort and so I take full responsibility for any technical or compositional errors. However, I have been very fortunate to have the expert support of my good friend, the photographer and founder member of the Maldon Archaeological Group, Geoff Clark (and his wife, Pauline), who has produced some of the best pictures for the book. Another friend, Hayley Trowbridge, has also supplied some of the present-day shots. District and Town Councillor, Mark Heard, kept my spirits up when I had doubts about being able to complete this project. In addition, I am grateful to the following for the loan of material and for their valuable contributions; Peter & Julie Hedge; Jean Whitaker; Kevin Fuller; Alan Wills; Ed and Brenda Joslin; Chris Cork; my cousins, Michael Emmett and Jonathon Yuill; and my mother Ann and her husband Les Puttock.

Above all, I would like to yet again acknowledge my long suffering wife, Christine, and our daughter, Catherine, for putting up with years of my ramblings about Maldon's history. This book represents my latest contribution to describing Maldon's rich, unique and very special heritage. I hope I have done it justice.

Time Travel
Come with us on this charabanc journey around the historic highways and byways of Maldon and Heybridge.

Introduction

Maldon is situated on high ground, overlooking the length of its tidal river – the Blackwater. Those natural features encouraged the earliest settlers, with habitation evidence from the Bronze Age onwards. To the north is Heybridge ('high bridge'), a separate place linked to Maldon by the 'Causeway', a track which originally crossed marshland. On the western edge of town is the rural hamlet of Beeleigh (a 'clearing in the trees where bee-hives are kept'). The great glory of Maldon was and still is its river, which has had a direct influence on the area's development and prosperity.

By the time of the Roman invasion, Iron Age tribal peoples were living on the hill, but the subsequent Romano–British colony was in Heybridge, where there was a 'civitas', or 'small town'. By the tenth century the principal occupation returned to the hill, then called 'Maeldune' – 'hill marked by a cross', or 'hill of assembly'. Edward the Elder built a 'burh' fortress there in 916 as a defence against the marauding Danes. This would have contained the town mint and survived at least one siege in 920, but finally fell as a result of the famous Battle of Maldon of 991 (commemorated in a poem of the same name). Maldon and Heybridge (then known as 'Tidwoldington' – literally 'Tid's town') both feature in the Domesday Survey of 1085/86 but as quite distinct places. At that stage Maldon was substantial, second only in importance to nearby Colchester. Its earliest known charter was issued under Henry II in 1171. As well as granting rights and privileges, this confirmed a requirement for the town to provide a horse for the army and a ship of war.

The Christian faith was embedded in the area by Saint Cedd in the seventh century and monasticism arrived with the establishment of a Premonstratensian Abbey at Beeleigh in 1180 and a Carmelite Friary in the heart of town in 1292. A Leper Hospital was built c. 1164, as well as the parish churches – All Saints (in the thirteenth century), St Peter's (united with All Saints in 1244), St Mary's, the 'Fisherman's church' (eleventh century) and St Andrew's, Heybridge (twelfth century). The Medieval core of Maldon centred on High Street, with shops and a number of specialist markets. The Moot Hall, originally at the head of the market place, moved to the former (fifteenth century) private home of the D'Arcy family in 1576. High Street extends to Church Street and the 'Hythe' ('haven' or 'safe place') fronting the river. Thomas Cammock gave the first convenient public water supply in 1587. He is one of a number of founding fathers, including: Ealdorman Brythnoth, of 991 battle fame; Robert Mantell, benefactor of All Saints Church and Beeleigh Abbey; Sir Robert D'Arcy, of the Moot Hall; and Dr Thomas Plume, Archdeacon of Rochester, who by his will of 1704, left a library and gave money for the school. Equally famous was Edward Bright, the 'Fat Man of Maldon', who weighed in at approximately 44 stone when he died in 1750.

Fortunes declined from the mid-sixteenth century but improved from the late eighteenth century. The Chelmer and Blackwater Navigation (or canal) opened in 1797, but by-passed Maldon via Beeleigh, joining the river at the now popular attraction of Heybridge Basin. The river was equally busy and lucrative throughout the eighteenth and nineteenth centuries. Thames sailing barges carried a variety of cargos to and from town (including the distinctive 'stackies', or hay barges) and local fishing boats, called 'smacks', worked the waters from

Northey to Mersea Islands. The railway arrived in 1847 with two stations and lines to Witham and Woodham Ferrers, linked by a 'bow-string' viaduct. For many years the main employers were the iron-founders and agricultural manufacturers, E. H. Bentall, at Heybridge and the Maldon Iron Works, on the Causeway, along with the timber merchants, John Sadd and Sons, at Fullbridge ('muddy bridge'). Maldon Salt, extracted from the river since Roman times, remains popular around the globe. With the opening of the Promenade Park in 1895, Maldon also became a tourist destination for rest, relaxation and, from 1905, swimming in the former Lake.

The population of Maldon has grown steadily since the Great War, from about 6¼ thousand to double that figure today. The pictures in this book illustrate the emergence of that old Saxon settlement up on the hill into a flourishing Victorian and Edwardian municipal borough, whose underlying street scenes can still be experienced today.

Ancient Borough Arms
The three Plantagenet lions remind us of Maldon's Royal Borough connections. The ship indicates the town's historic duty to supply a vessel to the monarch at time of war.

CHAPTER 1

Maldon

Earl Brythnoth, 1907/2006
The town's most famous son was killed at the Battle of Maldon in 991. Nathaniel Hitch's 1907 interpretation of the great man at All Saints Church is in stark contrast to the modern bronze by the sculptor, John Doubleday, unveiled at the end of the Promenade Extension in 2006. Brythnoth's death undoubtedly represents the sunset on Maldon's old Saxon order.

The Burh, 1775

King Edward the Elder constructed Maldon's Burh Fortress in 916 as a defence against Danish invaders. The antiquarian, Joseph Strutt published this sketch of the site in 1775. All Saints Church spire indicates that it centred on today's London Road, with ramparts following the line of Beeleigh Road, Gate Street, Spital Road, across the grounds of St Peter's Hospital and around Beacon Hill. A section of inner defence can still be made out at the western end.

Lodge Road, *c.* 1910
This area continued to feature in military defence. The origins of Lodge Road date to the Napoleonic scare, when it was the track to an army barracks, 'The Lodge', built in 1807. The Congregational Manse was originally at no. 10. A brick wall once separated the road from the adjacent Dykes Chase – the 'dyke' of the Burh.

London Road, *c.* 1900

The main route in and out of town was literally the road to London. The long building on the left (Reed House) was once the location of Maldon Grammar School. Conditions and facilities in the old school were very poor and pupil numbers low. However, a new headmaster, the Revd Ryland, encouraged more boys to attend and lived to see the school relocate to new, state of the art premises, in Fambridge Road in 1907.

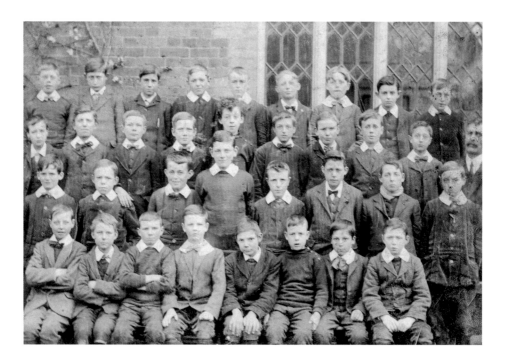

All Saints School, *c.* 1910

As well as the Grammar School, the National School (later All Saints Church of England Primary) also relocated to London Road. It cost £1,500 to build in 1847, using red bricks said to have been left over from the construction of the railway station. A dwelling for teachers was included at the front, with the boys' department to the right (as viewed from the road) and girls' to the left. The distinctive Elizabethan style windows can be seen in both this photograph of some of the pupils and in the surviving school house.

Soffe Family, 1900

Frederic J. and Robert J. Soffe lived with their parents at no 5 London Road (centre door). At the outbreak of the South African (or Boer) War in 1899, they enlisted for active service abroad. While Robert came home, Frederic died of fever at Blomfontein, on May 21 1900, whilst serving with the City of London Imperial Volunteers.

Inset: Frederic is remembered on an official CIV memorial in All Saints Church but also on this more personal brass plaque in St Mary's Church.

POLICE STATION WEST SQUARE, MALDON.

Police Station, 1912

Maldon's Police relocated from Moot Hall to a purpose built station in West Square in 1912. The site was previously a private garden owned by the Orttewell family who lived at Oakwood House opposite. PC Totterdell was on duty here in 1914 when a report came in of a ghost in Wantz Road – it turned out to be a sleep-walker!

Wentworth House, c. 1890

This yellow brick Victorian house in West Square was formerly the home of Miss A. L. Hutley. There were extensive grounds to the rear where, along with her gardener, Arthur Frederick Nunn (1900–1968), she nurtured a special Iris Reticulata.

Inset: Iris Reticulata 'Wentworth' selected for trial by the Royal Horticultural Society at Wisley in 1938.

High Street, Maldon.

High Street, 1911

When this view looking back to Wentworth House was taken, the site of the police station was still a garden. The building that now includes Stems the florist was the home of the Tew brothers, who ran a tearoom there and manufactured beehives. Opposite with the swinging sign was 'Ye Olde Tobaconist', specialising in snuff and cigars. Alice Gepp would have run the place at that stage.

High Street, Maldon

High Street, c. 1830

A number of buildings at the top of the High Street retain their Georgian façades, incorporating distinctive bays, broad doorways, steps and elaborate wrought iron hand rails. Nos. 15 (on the immediate left), 22 'Stonecroft', 24 and 24A (on the right) were originally private residences, rather than commercial premises. Early nineteenth century Maldon was a place of busy inns, Whig politics and shops selling everything from the latest books to silks and lace.

White Horse, 1903

The Bell Inn changed its name to the White Horse in about 1715. No. 26 High Street was then re-built, or at least re-fronted, towards the end of the eighteenth century. Local horse-drawn carriers once operated from here and a section of cobbled surface still survives at the entrance to the stableyard. James Stick was the landlord when this picture was taken in 1903 and he ran the place until 1917. Maldon Football Club also used it as their headquarters from 1914.

13.

All Saints Church, *c.* 1900

The eastern end of the row of shops originally extending right across the front of All Saints Church can still be seen in this view. They were finally removed in 1917. The thirteenth-century triangular tower, surmounted by an hexagonal spire, is unique and the Sanctus bell on the outside originally rang the town curfew. The beautiful south aisle dates to around 1330 and since 1907 its niches have contained statues of the town's founding fathers.

Inset: One of the shops in front of All Saints was the Maldon Meat Company (at no. 29).

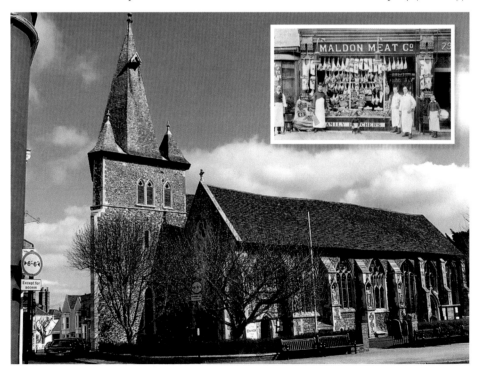

19

All Saints Church, c. 1920

A special (timeless) feature of All Saints is the beautiful fourteenth-century south aisle arcading, complete with Purbeck marble piers. The 1867 pulpit has since been replaced and the 1902 font repositioned, but the 1866 eagle lectern remains in place and the pews and organ pipes mirror their ancestors. A wooden chancel screen was later added, but has now also been moved – to the opening of the south chapel.

Cammock Memorial, 1895

Thomas Cammock (1540-1602) provided Maldon with its first convenient water supply. In 1587 he paid for a lead conduit to connect his well in Beeleigh Road to a pump on Cromwell Hill. Cammock married twice and fathered twenty-two children. His family monument in All Saints Church was illustrated in 1895 and you can still get close up to the great man today.

Inset: The well and pump as they appeared in 1993.

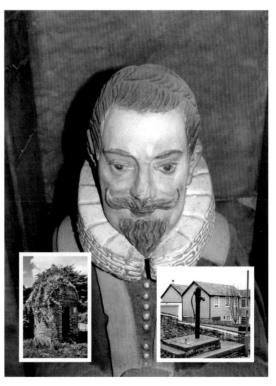

War Memorial, 1921

The town's Portland stone monument to the fallen of the Great War was unveiled by General Horne at 3 p.m. on May 8 1921, to the sound of a muffled peal from the All Saints bells. There was a large crowd of locals, relatives and ex-servicemen in attendance to remember the 146 dead. In 2011 two additional plaques were added, listing a further 102 names missing from the original memorial.

Inset: One of the new plaques.

Ted Last, 1914

One of the names on the memorial is William Edward (Ted) Last. The Census tells us that in 1901 he lived with his parents and older brother at 3 Gate Street. In 1914 both boys joined the army to fight for King and Country. Ted served as a Lance Corporal with the 2nd Battalion of the Essex Regiment. Whilst his brother survived (albeit minus an arm) Ted was killed in action near Arras on the morning of 28 March 1918.

Inset: The Last family home.

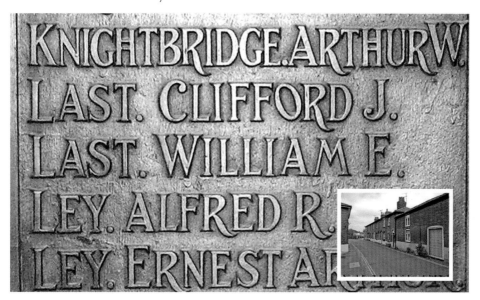

International Stores, 1913

The International (Tea Company) Stores took over 34 High Street in 1894. For four years prior to that it had been the premises of the Indian Empire Tea Company. In more recent times it has been a baker's – firstly Tooks, then The Baker's Oven and now Greggs. While the frontage has changed, the three eighteenth-century windows on the first floor identify the location.

High Street, 1913

On the eve of the Great War, what is now the Oak House bar at number 35 was two separate businesses – Guiver's 'Fancy Repository' and the (relocated) London Central Meat Company. Next door at 37 was Richard Poole's shop. He was a printer, stationer, bookseller and newsagent. Since the early 1970s the property has been divided into two but it is still called Poole House.

The Moot Hall, 1895

D'Arcy's Tower was built by Sir Robert D'Arcy in *c.* 1420, but was purchased by the town for use as their Moot Hall in 1576. It subsequently served as a charterhouse, council chamber, common hall, court, prison and police station. It was re-fronted and a portico added in 1810. The clock was installed in 1881 and railings in 1905. It is now managed by a 'Friends Group' and is licensed to hold weddings and civil partnerships.

Inset: William Shakespeare is said to have performed in the Hall in 1603.

Maldon Murderer, 1814/1988

On 27 October 1814 an inquest was held at the Moot Hall into the death of local milkman, William Belsham. It was found that he was the subject of a vendetta murder by Maldon sailor, William Seymour, who lately returned from sea. Seymour was sentenced to death and executed. In the 1980s the author was allowed access to a damaged painting of the murderer, then in store at Maldon Museum. On public display at that time was Seymour's skull.

King's Head Hotel, Maldon.

King's Head, *c.* 1900

38 High Street is no longer a public house, but this small courtyard shopping centre retains the King's Head name. The building itself dates back to the 1540s, with an older core as early as 1450. It was a popular coaching inn and became a very select place indeed with its own residential accommodation. Guests were met from East Station by the horse-drawn taxi service shown in this view. The owner, Mr Taylor, stands at the main entrance and portico.

THE SURPRISEING BETT DECIDED.

A View of Deciedeing the Wager between Mr. Codd and Mr. Hants of Maldon in the County of Efsex. which was that 7 Men where actually with great ease on the first day of December 1750 in the House of the Widow Day the Black Bull in Maldon aforesaid, button'd within the Waistcoat of Mr. Bright deceased.

Edward Bright, 'Fat Man of Maldon', 1750

Edward Bright was born in town in 1721. He weighed; 10 stone at age twelve and a half years; 24 stone at nineteen and a half; 41 stone at twenty-three; and 44 stone 6lbs when he died of Typhus, aged twenty-nine. A bet was made that 'seven hundred' men could fit into his waistcoat. Seven residents of lands known as the Dengie Hundred duly obliged. These contemporary engravings explain the story. The modern bronze on the wall of Continental Coffee at the King's Head Centre is by local artist, Catharni Stern.

After the Fire, 1893

During the night of Sunday 17 January 1892, a fire swept away a substantial section of the High Street. Ancient timber-framed buildings located between the Public Hall (at 43 and 45) and the draper's, W. Archer, on the corner of Market Hill (61) were destroyed. Replacement properties were constructed during 1892 and 1893, apart from numbers 49–51. The gap is still evident in this view.

Inset: Date plaque above numbers 57 and 59.

Post Office, 1907
49-51 High Street was eventually in-filled in 1907 in a striking mock-Tudor style. Maldon's post office was located here until 1980.

Gowers, Ltd., Maldon.

High Street, 1902

Edgar Harvey was a 'family draper, silk mercer, milliner, carpet warehouseman and undertaker', who also sold 'highclass boots and shoes'. In 1902 he acquired nos. 56 and 58 High Street from Bentall & Son. Today the shops have been separated for use by Cancer Research and Superdrug. Next door, at 54, was Thomas Pollard Petchey, Chemist, and the premises still perform that same function today as Boots.

St Peter's Church, *c.* 1910

St Peter's was ecclesiastically united with All Saints as early as 1244. Although it continued to function as a place of worship, it gradually became redundant and fell into disrepair. By 1665 the nave had collapsed and was then replaced by Dr Thomas Plume's red brick building to house his library and the grammar school. In this view the tower is in need of attention and has a tie band around it.

Inset: Dr Plume (statue at All Saints Church).

The Shears Monument, *c.* 1890
Since the Georgian period a prominent feature of St Peter's churchyard has been the tomb to the Shears family. William Shears, a local stone mason, died in 1817 and is remembered here along with his wife, Ann (died 1829) and their youngest daughter, Elizabeth (died 1818). Their Greek revival monument originally had a classical urn on top, which can just be seen behind the gas lamp in this view from the late nineteenth century.

Market Hill, Maldon.

Market Hill, 1910

Throughout the Tudor period this was the site of the butter market. From 1910 Percy Daniels had his draper's shop at no. 61 (now Coes of Maldon). It had been re-built in 1882, following another (earlier) High Street fire. The timber-framed building behind the ladies with their bikes was the Maldon Cycle Company and other businesses included a butcher's, a grocer's and a wine and spirit merchant. Since the 1920s this area has been continually re-developed, culminating in the construction of today's town hall.

Congregational Church, 1924

The present Congregational (URC) building was constructed in 1801 but was re-fronted in the 1860s. The prominent tomb in the foreground was removed in 1965 and the area now serves as a car park. The red brick building to the left originally housed the British School, forerunner to Maldon Primary, now in Wantz Road.

Richard Poole's Schooldays, 1840s

Local printer and headmaster's son, Richard Poole Jnr. (1834–1920) attended the British School during the 1840s. In his later memoires (of 1902) he recalls carving his initials on one of the bricks in the SW corner and, in his own words; '...my initials are still plainly visible thereon'.

Inset: There is also evidence of the sharpening of many slate pencils.

Hill House, *c.* 1910

This imposing building was originally the home of the Sadd family, who made their fortune as local timber merchants. The belvedere allowed them to view the movement of their products on their fleet of sailing barges on the River Blackwater. The property was eventually left to the Borough and became the Council Offices. Today it is an exclusive residential complex.

Inset: Henrietta Sadd (1863–1932) established a 'Home of Rest for Young Women' in the grounds.

Market Hill, 1905

Until 1873 the imposing building on the left was the town's Union Workhouse. It has since been converted into apartments. The housing on the immediate right was partly demolished in the 1930s and is now a pleasant municipal garden, offering a welcome rest to those making their way up the hill.

Maldon: The Wharf

Fullbridge, c. 1890

The section of the River Chelmer immediately above Fullbridge has always been one of the industrial centres of town. Barges would load and off-load at the numerous mills and timber works located there and on the right can be seen the now long-gone Rutt & Gutteridge Lime Kiln. Fullbridge continues to be a busy place and is home to Greens Flour and boatyards repairing a wide variety of vessels.

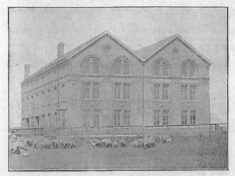

The Causeway Iron Works, 1895
Joseph Warren had his Maldon Iron Works foundry built in 1875. Countless ploughs, wagons, sack barrows, fencing and sign posts were made here. The company was in direct competition with Bentall's of Heybridge and were major employers until they were bought out by John Sadd & Sons Ltd in 1947. Sadd's stopped using the building in 1981 and it is now a gym, pizza takeaway, flooring specialist and cash exchange.

Inset: Thomas Nunn (1835–1905) was employed as a turner at the Iron Works.

Maldon. East Station.

Maldon East Station *c.* 1910

Maldon's former railway originally had two stations – West and East (& Heybridge). The latter was built in this grand Jacobean style in 1848, as part of a political bribe involving a railway director who was a parliamentary candidate for the Borough. The Maldon Branch Line and station finally closed in 1966.

Inset: Fred Bennett was the Maldon East (& Heybridge) signalman.

Fullbridge Street, 1923

At one time there were numerous businesses in this busy part of town. Arthur J. Dykes had his eartherware shop nearest right. Next to it was the White Hart – just one of a surprisingly large number of hostelries in the area that included near neighbour, the Welcome Sailor, and, in the distance, The Ship (right) and White Lion, offering 'good stabling' (left).

Fullbridge, 1832
This popular view of the Fullbridge/Market Hill route back into town includes some artistic licence. However, it records that the Welcome Sailor was originally The Angel. There have been a succession of bridges at this important river crossing and the 'Fulebridge' (literally 'muddy bridge') appears in the records of the Knights Templar in 1185.

Railway Viaduct, *c.* 1900/2006

Another river crossing closer to Beeleigh was constructed for the railway line extension in 1889. The former bow-string viaduct linked Maldon East (& Heybridge) with Maldon West and the route to Woodham Ferrers. The viaduct became redundant with the closure of the Maldon Branch Line and it was finally replaced by the bypass bridge in 1990.

MARKET HILL, MALDON.

The Ship, *c.* 1900

By the eighteenth century the Ship (on the right) was renowned as a place of hospitality and entertainment. It became a minor staging post and offered 'good beds and stabling'. By the time this picture was taken it was serving 'Salts Burton Ales'. John Wood was the landlord and Maldon Angling Club used the place as their headquarters. It finally closed as a pub in 1961 and is now private flats.

Inset: A 'Tramp's Supper' at the Ship sometime between 1954 and 1956.

High Street, Maldon.

High Street, 1906

Opposite the Swan stands an important row of ancient buildings (nos. 92 to 100). Albert Fulcher, a sewing machine agent, was at 92. No. 94 does not look commercial, but a boot maker (John Marrison) was there in 1913. Nos. 96 and 98 again look like private dwellings, although there was a greengrocer (Henry Pugh) at 98 from 1910. Alfred Lucking, farmer and cattle dealer, lived at 100, but this was swept away with other properties in 1927 to make way for the Hippodrome Picture Palace.

Wantz Corner, 1905

This grocer's shop on the corner of Wantz Road and High Street, was destroyed in another terrible fire during the night of the 14 January 1910. The replacement building, houses Reeve's well known traditional ironmongery business with the Maldon Cookshop next door. The large building with the bay windows beyond is 'The Gables', formerly a private house, doctor's surgery, school, hotel and then a children's home. Today it is 'Intimo', a contemporary restaurant.

Butt Lane, *c.* 1900

The Baptist Chapel was constructed in Butt Lane (the former route to the town's archery grounds) in 1896. The mayor, Leonard Bentall, Thomas and Joseph Sadler and the minister, Revd Morris, each laid foundation stones. It cost £1,821 10s 7½d and was built by A. Baxter & Son to the designs of P. M. Beaumont. A school extension was added in 1914 and promptly requisitioned as a military hospital for twenty-five beds.

Victoria Road, Maldon.

Victoria Road, 1916

This road was developed in the late Victorian period for middle class residential use. The occupations of those living there included insurance agents, builders, a registrar, postmaster and borough engineer.

Inset: An 1897 advert for remaining building plots.

VICTORIA ROAD
BUILDING ESTATE
MALDON.

There are still a few Plots for sale in good positions on this charming Estate which is the nearest to the

MARINE PROMENADE,
And, standing very high, commands Lovely Views for many miles over River and Field.

ROADS MADE, SEWERED, GAS and WATER MAINS LAID.

Possession on payment of 10 per cent.

BALANCE BY QUARTERLY PAYMENTS IF DESIRED.

FREE CONVEYANCES.

If preferred, Plots may be hired on 99 years Building Lease.

Solicitors: Surveyor:
Messrs. Beaumont & Bright,   F. M. Beaumont, Esq., A.M.I.C.E.,
Maldon.   Maldon.

Agents for the Estate :

Messrs. SPURGEON & SON,
52, HIGH STREET, MALDON,
Of whom sizes and particulars may be obtained.

Gas Works, c. 1883

Sir Claude Champion de Crespigney, 4th Baronet, of Champion (now Totham) Lodge, Broad Street Green was described as a 'plucky individual'. One of his many passions was ballooning and, along with his assistant, 'Aeronaut Simmons', made a number of launches from a field near the Gas Works in Victoria Road. On one occasion they made a successful trip to Holland. The Gas Works site looks quite different now.

Inset: Sir Claude (1847–1935).

Warwick Arms, c. 1920/1986

The Warwick Arms at 185 High Street, on the corner of Victoria Road, was originally called the Queen Adelaide. It was re-named in 1899, probably after the Earl of Warwick who, as Provincial Grand Master of the Freemasons of Essex, had visited Maldon three years earlier. It has since been known as Reflections, The Yardarm and Clarkies, but thankfully the Earl was then remembered again.

The Embassy Cinema, 1936

Local labour was engaged by Messrs. Smith of Norwood to build the long, three-storied King George's Place. The new complex included a cinema, designed by the young architect, David Nye, for Shipman & King Cinemas Ltd. The workforce is photographed here in front of what would become the 'Embassy'. After a mixed history the cinema was finally demolished in 1985 to make way for Embassy Court retirement flats.

Primative Methodist Church, *c.* 1900
National quarrels within the Methodist movement resulted in a series of schisms and the establishment of different 'Connexions'. This chapel at the top of Wantz Road was built in 1860 to accommodate 300 Primative Methodists. Now minus its spire, today it is the local corps and community centre (or citadel) for the Salvation Army.

Inset: Maldon's Salvation Army Band outside the Congregational Church in 1934.

'Mizpah', 1908

The end house of this ivy-clad terrace in Wantz Road (no 48) was once called 'Mizpah' – a biblical reference to a bond between separated people. From 1902 it was Miss H. J. Sadd's 'Home of Rest for Young Women'. In 1922 it became the 'Middleton Home for the Blind', under the supervision of a Miss M. Gallagher. Today it is the Middleton Manor Residential Care Centre.

Wantz Road, _c._ 1900

Nearly half a mile long and running south off High Street, Wantz Road gets its name from the High German _gantz_ – 'the pointing hand', or 'the four want ways'. On the right is the junction with Queen Street and opposite is Dyers Road. The weather-boarded building on the left is the Volunteer Arms, opened in the 1860s and where time was finally called in 1979.

Fambridge Road, *c.* 1918.

Originally known as Pinchgut Hall Lane, after an isolation hospital, Fambridge Road was literally the way to Fambridge and the ferry over the River Crouch. Here local woodman, Austin George Hedge (1856–1926) stands outside his terraced house, next to a cart, driven by his son, Harold Victor Hedge (1903–1974). The terrace had earlier contained a beer house called the Red Cow, opened in the 1850s, but closed by 1910.

Maldon Grammar School, 1931/2006

The town's grammar school relocated from London Road to purpose built premises on the Fairfield, off Fambridge Road in 1907. Sydney Deed was headmaster from 1912 to 1939 and the additional hall and library wing were not added until 1932. The central tower later had a clock and light added as a remembrance to former pupils killed in both world wars. It became a comprehensive school in 1970 and continues as the successful Plume Academy.

Maldon Air Training Corps, 1944/1974

Number 1207 Squadron Air Training Corps was formed in 1941 and had close associations with Maldon Grammar School. The head of science, W. Harry Bream, was commanding officer and second-in-charge was geography teacher, Donald Brierley. The cadets included some of their pupils. 1207 was disbanded after hostilities, but was re-formed and, throughout the 1970s, to the present day continues to meet in the drill hall in Tenterfield Road.

The Union House, Maldon.

The Workhouse, 1919

Maldon's Union House opened in Spital Road in 1873. It was designed by the architect, Frederick Peck, and constructed by the suitably Dickensian sounding Ebenezer Saunders, for £21,500. Male, female and child inmates were segregated and spent much of their time breaking rocks for the roads. Today the building houses the very caring St Peter's Hospital.

Inset: On Tuesday 22nd April 1884, at exactly 9.17 a.m. by the Workhouse clock, an earthquake was felt across town.

Hospital Chapel, 1943
The former Workhouse chapel, with its distinctive windows, served as a mortuary during the Second World War. Here are the personnel of the Civil Defence (ARP) St Peter's Fixed First Aid Post. The small man nearest the front is Charles Lavender, who was killed in an accident following an air raid on the town in 1944.

Spital Road, 1915
Maldon suffered a Zeppelin raid on Friday 16 April 1915. Two bombs and twenty 16lb incendiaries were dropped across town. Thankfully there were no casualties but a workshop in Spital Road was completely destroyed. Stalwart little Rose Cottage survived and serves as a reminder of the event.

Zeppelin Raid on Maldon

Arthur Smith's Workshop, 1915

The Spital Road workshop and iron shed destroyed in the Zeppelin raid of 1915 belonged to the builder, Arthur Smith. Damage was also caused to neighbouring buildings and windows were broken in nearby Mount Pleasant. Apart from the end of Rose Cottage and the position of the telegraph pole, the scene is now unrecognisable.

Inset: One of the incendiary bombs.

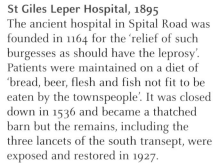

St Giles Leper Hospital, 1895
The ancient hospital in Spital Road was
founded in 1164 for the 'relief of such
burgesses as should have the leprosy'.
Patients were maintained on a diet of
'bread, beer, flesh and fish not fit to be
eaten by the townspeople'. It was closed
down in 1536 and became a thatched
barn but the remains, including the
three lancets of the south transept, were
exposed and restored in 1927.

CHAPTER 2

The Riverside

Church Street, c. 1890

An amazing range of houses, of different sizes and of varying heights and roof lines, on the southern side of Church Street, were swept away in the 1920s as part of so called 'town slum clearance number 1'. They were replaced by the current terrace, ending at number 24 nearest St Mary's. The sign opposite marks the former 'Star' beerhouse, run by James Wager from 1893.

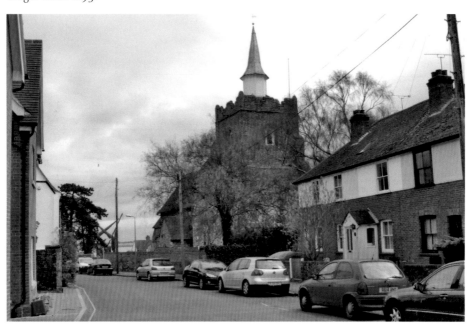

Church Street, 1945
Church Street residents celebrated VE Day outside what was then the Salvation Army Hall. Since that time the little building has served as a Labour Hall and is today the centre of the Maldon District Islamic Cultural Association.

St Mary's Church, c. 1880/1900

St Mary's (the Fishermans' Church) was built in about 1130, but undoubtedly stands on the site of much earlier churches, possibly dating back to as early as the seventh century. It formerly just consisted of the twelfth century nave, tower of 1300 (partly re-built 1628) and shortened chancel of 1720. However extension work to the south, under the direction of Frederick Chancellor, saw the addition of an aisle and vestry in 1886.

St Mary's Church, 1990/Present Day

Until relatively recent times, the outside appearance of the church remained very much as it did following the additional building work of 1886. The late Father Andrew McIntosh was then responsible for the construction of the 'Octagon' in 1992, which provided a meeting room and social space for parishioners and friends.

Jolly Sailor, *c.* 1950

The rear, timber-framed section, of the Jolly Sailor pub in Church Street dates from the end of the sixteenth century. The building has served as a hostelry since about 1800. Throughout the 1940s and 1950s it was the haunt of local fishermen. Here Walter Pitt (1882–1971) leaves his house at no. 57 and makes his way down the hill for a swift half.

    Inset: Landlord and landlady, Mr and Mrs Everitt, behind the bar in the 1950s.

Hythe Quay, c. 1890
'Hythe' is Anglo-Saxon for 'haven' and has been a safe mooring since at least the tenth century. For over 100 years it has been the home berth of Thames Sailing Barges. *Minerva*, seen here against the backdrop of St Mary's, was built in 1854 and was a competitor in the early barge matches. Today, Topsail Charters operate trips from the Hythe with their vessels; *Thistle* (1895), *Hydrogen* (1906), and (seen here) *Reminder* (1929).

River Blackwater, showing Fishing Smacks, Maldon.

Bath Wall Moorings, *c.* 1920

Maldon once had a veritable fleet of 'smacks' – sailing vessels used for fishing and developed to near perfection by the Essex fishermen and shipbuilders. They were mainly moored alongside the Bath Wall, on the edge of the Promenade. Amongst their number was MN12 *Polly*, still going strong but today based at Brightlingsea.

Sailing MN12 *Polly*, 1940s/2009

From her construction at Maldon in the late nineteenth century by master shipwright, John Howard, until she was sold to the late John Kemp in 1956, *Polly* was owned and worked by the Pitt family of Church Street. Here Ernie Pitt (1874–1959) brings her home after a day's fishing. Some seventy years later the author (a Pitt descendant) takes the tiller.

   Inset: The sleek lines of *Polly*.

Bath Wall Parliament, *c.* 1950/2010
Successive generations of Maldon fishermen used to meet on a bench next to an old tin shed alongside the Bath Wall. Known as the Bath Wall (or Tin Shed) Parliament, they are now long gone. However, a memorial bench and explanatory display board attached to a replacement shed now mark the spot.

PROMENADE GATES, MALDON.

Promenade Gates, 1925

Promenade Park opened to the public on the 26 June 1895. The main entrance consists of two wrought-iron pedestrian gates and a double-gated vehicular access, originally flanked by gas lamps. The Lodge (at 47 Mill Road) was built for the Park Superintendent in 1915 and now houses the Maldon Museum.

Promenade Tea Rooms, *c.* 1920

Clement Last purchased the Promenade Refreshment Rooms from the Handley family in 1911. He provided Lyons teas, Fry's and Cadbury's chocolates, Captain cigarettes and sold souvenirs. The family lived in the adjacent Promenade Villa and Clement's son, James Clement, took over the business in the early 1930s, remaining there until 1967. Today it is a private house.

The Lake, 1912

The swimming lake was opened on the Promenade on the 23 June 1905. A staggering 9,000 people were present that day to mark the start of what would be many decades of enjoyment by generations of locals and visitors alike. It was a huge tourist attraction throughout the summer months. However, it is no longer used for swimming, but has become an attractive haven for wildlife.

The Promenade, Maldon.

Promenade, c. 1920

This view along what would become known as the 'Extension' pre-dates the enlargement works of 1925 and 1926. The town bandstand seen here was subsequently moved nearer to the Lake in 1922 and the white shed in the distance on the left was a men's changing room for river swimming. The Hedgecock family operated boat hire and pleasure trips from this part of the river.

CHAPTER 3

Beeleigh

Beeleigh Road, Maldon.

Beeleigh Road, 1906

The route out of town to the hamlet of Beeleigh is along this road, which links Silver Street to the footpath around the back of the Lodge and the top of Constitutional Hill. The rows of terrace cottages here are almost entirely of nineteenth-century origin and the road was described as 'comparatively modern' in 1895.

Beeleigh Abbey, *c.* 1900

Retired Indian civil servant, John Doyle Field, moved into the semi-ruinous Beeleigh Abbey in about 1890. He took a keen interest in the history of the building, but his real passion was the garden, noted for its climbing roses. He can be seen here in white jacket and hat talking to a visitor. The place looks much improved today – both the house and garden!

Inset: Doyle Field's grave in nearby Maldon Cemetery.

Beeleigh Abbey, *c.* 1900
For a long while the post-Dissolution timber-framed addition to the abbey was thought to date to about 1540. However, modern analysis suggests it wasn't constructed until 1624. Like the rest of the building, it has recently undergone extensive, sympathetic, award winning restoration.

Chapter House Entrance, *c.* 1922
Beeleigh Abbey's Chapter House is a remarkable survival, particularly as it served as a cattle shed until 1912. Built in about 1220, it was originally the place where the canons met to listen to a daily chapter reading from their Rule. The processional entrance is seen here in two views divided by some ninety years.

Cloister Wing, 1903

The surviving east wing of the abbey cloister consists of (left to right): the reredorter (toilets); upper floor dorter (sleeping quarters) with calefactory below (warming room); small parlour; and chapter house. The later section had partly collapsed by the time this picture was taken but was carefully reconstructed in 1912.

Lion Avenue, Maldon Nº 1664.

Lion Avenue, 1918

This was once Beeleigh's main street, with housing either side and the water corn mill at the end. It takes its name from the Lion Tree, a diseased elm with a growth on the side that resembled a lion's head. The tree was a major attraction, but had to be felled to a stump in 1918. The stump was then removed in 1934, but the name of the avenue remains.

Beeleigh Falls Walk, Maldon.

The Lily Pond, 1908

The headwater channel, or mill stream, became redundant following the destruction of Beeleigh Mill by a fire in 1875. However, it was then converted into an ornamental pond, famous for 'Moore's beautiful virgin lily'. In 1970 the pond was, in turn, backfilled as part of a willow planting scheme.

Lovers Walk, Beeleigh

Lovers' Walk, 1925
All of the lanes and paths in Beeleigh have
a name. The track that links the Stepped
Weir with the Long Weir is called Lovers'
Walk and originally had fenced bridges and
a number of 'kissing gates'.

Beeleigh Falls, c. 1905

The Long Weir next to the Chelmer and Blackwater Navigation was described in the nineteenth century as 'Maldon's Niagara Falls'! The weir takes flood water from the tributary of the Blackwater coming through Langford and lets it into the Flood Hole and then to the tidal Chelmer. It can still be an impressive sight after heavy rain.

CHAPTER 4

Heybridge

Heybridge, 1924

This procession, complete with marching band, is leaving Heybridge over the River Blackwater Bridge and heading for the Causeway. The Half Moon pub can be seen in the distance and the gable end of the Anchor is opposite, advertising spirits, luncheons and teas. The cycle engineer, Jack Hunter, had his garage just beyond the pub yard.

Heybridge Square, *c.* 1910

The lamp and frontage of the Half Moon can again be seen in this picture. Beyond it was the boarding house for apprentices employed at E. H. Bentall & Sons, agricultural engineering works. The shop nearest the camera, with the cart outside, was Harrington's, the grocer's.

St Andrew's Church, 1906

The vicarage seen in this view was demolished and replaced in 1908. However, the very unusual squat tower of St Andrew's Church, with pyramidal roof, has changed very little. This particular feature of the church is a product of a collapse and 'capping-off' during the mid to late fifteenth century.

The Towers, 1920/2006

Edward Hammond Bentall (1814–1898) built the Towers as his family seat in 1873. It was constructed in an Italianate style out of concrete blocks and stood in its own landscaped garden, complete with lake. Subsequently used as a convalescent home, a prisoner of war camp and then council accommodation, it was demolished in the 1950s. It has been replaced with a housing estate, but the surviving gate lodge reminds us of its former glory.

Canal from Wave Bridge, Heybridge.

The Canal, 1910
This view from Wave Bridge shows a horse-drawn lighter heading along the straight cut of the navigation towards the Basin. On the right is the mighty Bentall warehouse, built in 1863 to store finished products ready for shipping to destinations across the globe.

Canal Moorings, 1926

For many years this section of the Chelmer and Blackwater Navigation towards the Heybridge Basin end has been a popular mooring for yachts. Access to the River Blackwater is by way of the Basin lock just a short distance away.

Heybridge Basin, 1909

Until 1793 this area was an obscure piece of marshland. The settlement then sprang up around the lock, linking the new navigation with Collier's Reach in the River Blackwater. The weather-boarded cottages date from that early period, but the Old Ship (formerly the Chelmer Brig) was enlarged and re-opened as a pub in 1906.